ELT Graded Readers

UPPER INTERMEDIATE

SHAKESPEARE'S THEATRE

Written by David Maule

Series Editor Susan Holden

A Dorling Kindersley Book

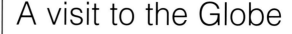

A visit to the Globe

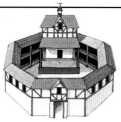

The Globe
The word "globe" means world. The playhouse had a sign on the wall explaining its name. This said: "This whole world is a stage."

It is the summer of 1602 and you are a visitor to London. Most of the city lies on the north side of the River Thames. Here, there are many things to do and see. There are fine buildings like the Palace of Westminster, St Paul's Cathedral and the Tower of London.

A cutpurse will explain how he learned his trade – stealing from people in the audience. See page 34.

Cuthbert Burbage, the company's businessman, will tell you all about his playhouse. See page 8.

A waterman will row you across the River Thames to the Globe. See page 6.

Nick Tooley, a boy actor, will tell you what it's like to play the women in Shakespeare's plays. See page 26.

To the reader:

Welcome to the DK ELT Graded Readers! These readers are different. They explore aspects of the world around us: its history, geography, science … and a lot of other things. And they show the different ways in which people live now, and lived in the past.

These DK ELT Graded Readers give you material for reading for information, and reading for pleasure. You are using your English to do something real. The illustrations will help you understand the text, and also help bring the Reader to life. There is a glossary to help you understand the special words for this topic. Listen to the cassette or CD as well, and you can really enter the world of the Olympic Games, the *Titanic*, or the Trojan War … and a lot more. Choose the topics that interest you, improve your English, and learn something … all at the same time.
Enjoy the series!

To the teacher:

This series provides varied reading practice at five levels of language difficulty, from elementary to FCE level:
BEGINNER
ELEMENTARY A
ELEMENTARY B
INTERMEDIATE
UPPER INTERMEDIATE
The language syllabus has been designed to suit the factual nature of the series, and includes a wider vocabulary range than is usual with ELT readers: language linked with the specific theme of each book is included and glossed. The language scheme, and ideas for exploiting the material (including the recorded material) both in and out of class are contained in the Teacher's Resource Book. We hope you and your students enjoy using this series.

Dorling **DK** Kindersley

LONDON, NEW YORK, SYDNEY, DELHI,
PARIS, MUNICH & JOHANNESBURG

Originally published as Dorling Kindersley
Reader *Welcome to The Globe – The Story of
Shakespeare's Theatre* in 2000 and adapted as
an ELT Graded Reader for
Dorling Kindersley by

studio **cactus** **c**

13 SOUTHGATE STREET WINCHESTER HAMPSHIRE SO23 9DZ

Published in Great Britain by
Dorling Kindersley Limited
9 Henrietta Street, London WC2E 8PS

2 4 6 8 10 9 7 5 3 1

Copyright © 2000
Dorling Kindersley Limited, London

ISBN 0-7513-2943-6

Colour reproduction by Colourscan, Singapore
Printed and bound in China by
L. Rex Printing Co., Ltd
Text film output by Chimera.trt, UK

The publisher would like to thank the following
for their kind permission to reproduce their photographs:
c=centre; t=top; b=below; l=left; r=right

Adam Butler/PA Photos, London: 46a; Atkinson Art Gallery,
Southport/Bridgeman Art Library, London: Billie Love
Historical Collection: 26, 36a, 38ar; Dulwich Picture Gallery,
London/Bridgeman Art Library, London: 20a; E.T. Archive,
London: 39a; Fitzwilliam Museum, University of Cambridge,
UK/Bridgeman Art Library, London: 34; Guildhall
Library/Bridgeman Art Library, London: 6, 10b; The Kobal
Collection, London: 47a; Mary Evans Picture Library: 8b, 13a,
14, 16a, 17, 25, 37, 38–39b, 44, 45; Philip Mould, Historical
Portraits Ltd, London/Bridgeman Art Library, London: 15; The
Raymond Mander & Joe Mitcheson Theatre Collection Ltd:
20b; Rex Features: 46a; © Sonia Halliday Photographs: 9b.
Jacket: Peter Dennis

See our complete catalogue at

www.dk.com

Contents

However, if you want some fun, it's better to cross the river to Bankside. This is where the playhouses are. The most famous of these is the Globe. It has the best actors – and these include Mr William Shakespeare.

You will meet a number of people. They will answer all your questions.

Kate Strong, the apple-seller, will explain why the Globe has to close down because of a disease called the plague. See page 38.

Henry Sackville, a gallant, will tell you how he comes to the playhouse to show off his expensive clothes. See page 28.

Richard Burbage, the greatest actor in England, will explain to you the tricks of the trade. See page 20.

Bankside
The area called Bankside was the entertainment centre of London during the time of Shakespeare.

A groundling, who pays a penny to watch the plays from the yard, will tell you how he enjoys himself at the Globe. See page 30.

The waterman

You'd like a boat? Here you are! Just step in – that's it. Now hold on to my arm and sit down. That's good. I can see you're not used to small boats. From the country, are you? You'll like London – there's lots to do and see. The river's busy today. That's better. It's good to get clear of the bank – the air's fresher out here. Yes, I've been a waterman for fifteen years now. I'll have you across in no time at all.

So you're new to the city, are you? Well, you'll find a lot of things to see on the South Bank. The Globe? Yes, that's a good choice. People say it's the best playhouse in London. I wouldn't know myself – never have time to go there. Well, I could, but when I'm not working I'd rather just have a drink or two with my friends. But the Globe is good, they say. That Richard Burbage – he's the leading actor – I hear he's the best in London. I had him in my boat one day.

London Bridge
Playgoers who could not afford the boat fare crossed over the River Thames using London Bridge – the only bridge over the river at the time.

A play today
Flags flew over the playhouses when there was to be a play that day. The playhouses were open to the air. Plays were not put on in bad weather, or if it looked like it might rain.

An old print of the Thames in London.

See those three flags over my shoulder? They're flying over the playhouses. The Globe is the biggest one. The other two are the Rose and the Swan. It's always good to see the flags flying. That means a lot of people want to be taken across the river.

Here we are. Why, thank you – very good of you. Now, you take care. Just put your foot here – that's it. Goodbye – and I hope you enjoy the play.

Water taxis
The London watermen were like today's taxi drivers, only on water. They took passengers up, down and across the River Thames. The river was usually crowded with boats of all sizes.

THAMESIS

Cuthbert
Cuthbert Burbage was the manager of the Globe. He played some parts on the stage, but was not as famous as his brother, Richard.

Travellers
When travelling actors came to town, they put up a stage in the market-place or in the courtyard of an inn. They set up at fairs, too.

Theatre business

Yes, this is my theatre. My name's Cuthbert Burbage and I built it with my brother, Richard.

When we were boys, there were no playhouses in England. Our father, James, was a travelling player, or actor, and became the head of his own company. They used to perform at inns. These were normally built in a square around an open space called the yard. This is where the coaches and horses came in. We used to arrive and build a stage up against one wall. The ordinary people stood in the yard and watched. People staying at the inn, or other locals who had some money, could watch from their rooms. After the show, we passed round a hat to collect money from the audience. Or sometimes they just threw money onto the stage.

For Richard and me, it was a good life. But you never knew how many people would turn up, or how much money they would give. So some people, like my father, had the idea of building permanent playhouses in London. They were quite similar to the inns, really. There was a space around the stage for people to stand, and seats inside the walls.

Father borrowed some money and built a
playhouse in Shoreditch, to the north of
the city. He called it the Theatre, from
the Greek word *theatron*, which means a
viewing place. This was to remind people
that acting is an old and respectable craft.

Greek theatre
The ancient
Greeks built the
first theatres 2,500
years ago. They
put on plays as
part of religious
celebrations.

Audiences
Playhouses could hold an audience of 2,000–3,000. People who went to see the plays included both the rich and the poor.

Our father ran the Theatre for many years, and he taught Richard and me all he knew about the business. As boys, we had to act the women's parts, because women were not allowed on the stage. We soon discovered that Richard had a great talent as a player. I used to act as well, but I was more interested in the business side. I still am.

The Theatre was a great success, perhaps more so than Father had imagined when he built it. Because it was permanent, people knew where to go to see a play and big crowds came along. And of course, because we owned the building, we could charge them money to get in.

But there was one problem. Father didn't own the land on which the Theatre was built. It belonged to a man called Giles Allen. Father had taken out a lease on it, which means that he had paid for the right to use it for 21 years. This ended in April 1597, and as that date approached, Giles Allen began to think that he could make some money out of us.

Playhouses
By 1597, there were four playhouses in London. One was Burbage's Theatre. The other three were the Rose, the Curtain and the Swan.

He demanded a fortune to renew the lease, more than Father could pay. In this way, he hoped to have our playhouse.

Father argued with Allen about the lease. It may be that all the worry and the arguments finished him, because he died suddenly, leaving Richard and me to sort things out. I was worrying about it one night, when suddenly the answer came to me. It was so simple.

A better job
Allen wrote that he wanted to use the wood of the playhouse for a better purpose.

11

At that time there were already some theatres to the south of the city, in Bankside. We went across there and leased a piece of land. Next, we hired some builders, and while everyone else was celebrating Christmas – this was in December 1598 – we began to take the Theatre apart.

It was a big job. Everything had to be loaded onto carts and pulled the three kilometres down Bishopsgate, then across London Bridge to Bankside. Once there, we started to build a new theatre. We called it the Globe. Giles Allen was very angry when he found out what we had done. We didn't care. It was his own fault. If he'd asked for a reasonable price, we would have paid it. Now all he had was an empty piece of land.

Five actor friends helped us to start the company: Will Kemp, Augustine Phillips, Tom Pope, John Hemming and Will Shakespeare. Richard and I own 50 per cent, and the other five own the rest between them. We are called the Sharers, because we share the profits. Of course, we share the costs, too.

English style
Most English buildings were made by fixing large pieces of wood together, then filling in the spaces. They could be taken to pieces quite easily.

Good company
As well as the Sharers, the company at the Globe included some musicians, hired actors and odd-job men, called stagekeepers.

13

No licence
Actors who performed without a lord's licence could be whipped or branded – marked on the face with a red-hot iron.

Disapproval
The Puritans didn't like dancing, music or plays. They believed that people should only work very hard and pray to God.

The law of England says that all actors need a lord or lady to give them permission to perform. We get ours from the Lord Chamberlain. He is responsible for all the organization of the royal palaces. He is a powerful man, and we are happy that our company can call itself "The Lord Chamberlain's Men".

We need our lord's protection, because we have many enemies. The chief among these are the Puritans. Back in my father's time, before I was born, England was ruled by Henry VIII. He got into a quarrel with the Pope, and the result was that he changed the religion of England from Roman Catholic to Protestant. Since then the Protestants have gradually divided into two groups. One of these is quite relaxed. They enjoy going to plays and other types of entertainment. The other group, the Puritans, seem to hate anything that people enjoy doing. They hate playhouses especially, because they believe we encourage people to forget the church.

The city of London is governed by people called aldermen. Most of them are Puritans and so they won't let us perform in the city. That's why there are now so many playhouses south of the river.

The aldermen can do nothing about the playhouses, but they often ask Queen Elizabeth to close them down, but she enjoys watching plays.
She doesn't come to Bankside, but we go to her palaces to perform at times like Christmas.

Queen Elizabeth in about 1600.

Comedies
Comedies such as *Twelfth Night* were light-hearted plays about love with happy endings. There was often a part for a dancer or clown.

Will's plays
Shakespeare wrote 38 plays. Most of them appeared in a book put together by his actor friends after his death in 1616.

Each of our players has his own speciality. My brother, Richard, always plays the main part, of course. Tom Pope is an acrobat. Will Kemp is very good at comic parts, and he's also a fine dancer. He's always popular with the audiences – I think sometimes he makes the others jealous.

Will Shakespeare is a good enough player, but the thing he's best at is writing plays. We put on up to 15 a month. Will doesn't have time to write them all, so we use a lot by other writers too – like Christopher Marlowe. His plays are still popular, even though he's been dead for … it must be ten years now. He was mixed up in politics in some way, and somebody killed him in a pub in Deptford. A pity, but the crowd still pays to see his plays – like *Tamburlaine the Great* and *Edward II*. Will says he's learned a lot from them. That's true, but most people think he'll never be as good as Kit Marlowe.

But Will can write all sorts of plays. His latest, *Twelfth Night*, is a comedy. Before that, he wrote some about the history of England. People love them because of the battles.

Last month, Will finished a new type of play, a tragedy called *Hamlet*. It went down well with the crowd. Will Kemp hated it, of course, because he couldn't fool around, but it attracted better-off people. We try to please all tastes.

Tragedies
Tragedies were about the sufferings of great heroes and heroines. They always ended with the death of the main character.

Histories
History plays about an English victory in battle were popular in wartime. The country was at war with Spain from 1585 until 1604.

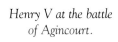

Henry V at the battle of Agincourt.

17

Costly clothes
Each playhouse had expensive costumes for their actors. A king's robe decorated with gold and silver probably cost more than a day's total income.

Quick change
The tiring house was used as a dressing room. Actors often had more than one part in a play, so they had to change into their costumes very quickly.

Would you like to have a look around the playhouse? Just follow me across the yard. This is where most of the audience are when the play is on. They're called the groundlings – because they stand on the ground. Even some richer people say it's more fun down here, and you can buy sweets and fruit from people walking around. But you have to keep the groundlings happy. If they don't like what they see, they sometimes throw the fruit at the actors.

Now, follow me up onto the stage. There are some rooms at the back here, and we call this place the tiring house. This is where we keep the costumes. We spend lots of money on these.

I get some clothes from the servants of rich people, who often give their old clothes away. Servants aren't allowed to wear things like that, so they sell them to us.

Look at this purple robe. Richard wears this when he plays a king.

Dress law
Everyone had to wear clothes according to their position in society. People whose clothes were thought to be too expensive were arrested and fined.

The star

Self-portrait
Richard Burbage
was a talented
painter as well as
an actor. This
picture may be his
self-portrait.

English hero
Henry V was king
of England from
1413 to 1422. He
attacked France in
1415 and had a
great victory over
the French army
at Agincourt.

Yes, I'm Richard Burbage. You've heard of me? Well, I *am* quite famous. Yes, Cuthbert, I know – I'm the greatest actor in all the playhouses. Now, why don't you go and add up the money again?

Cuthbert likes the business side of things more. I'm not so good at it. Did he tell you about our father? Yes, well, he was a good actor and a good manager as well. But it seems that Cuthbert and I got half of his nature each. It works well enough, provided we agree – and we do, most of the time.

So I play the big parts – kings, heroes, villains, madmen – I've played them all. And I love it, too. It's when I feel most alive, when I'm out there on the stage. Today, we're doing *Henry V* again. Will Shakespeare wrote it about three years ago, and it's been a favourite from the start. Very exciting – Henry V was a great English hero, and still is. He beat the French at the Battle of Agincourt.

It's one of the most popular plays with the crowd, but I wouldn't say it's my own favourite. There's a lot of shouting and waving swords and things like that, but it isn't very deep. I try not to overact. I shouldn't say this, but I've seen some actors really make a mess of parts like "Henry" – far too much noise. You need to try to imagine what the man was really like.

Lifelike
Many players overacted, waving their arms about and shouting. But Richard Burbage was famous for his realistic acting.

A scene is set
The actors had to set the scene. For example, a lighted candle showed it was night-time.

There are a lot of battle-scenes in *Henry V*. We try to make them as real as possible for the audience, and that isn't very easy with seven actors. So we have groups of actors rushing on and off the stage. They talk for a few seconds, and describe how the battle is going. That helps the audience to believe that it is really happening, but they can't see it.

Language
Shakespeare's words often helped audiences to understand. The characters might describe night falling, day breaking or the wind blowing.

Of course, anybody who isn't on stage is behind the scenes, shouting and beating drums, or maybe hitting swords together. I tell you, acting in a battle-scene in a playhouse is probably as tiring as taking part in a real one.

And when we fight on the stage, we come on from one side and move across quickly. It's all part of the trick. As well as that, we try to get the audience to use their imagination. At the beginning we say, "Let us on your imaginary forces work," and "Think when we talk of horses that you see them."

In one of the scenes, we show the English army attacking a French city. You noticed the balcony at the back of the stage? Well, we pretend that's the city wall. While I make my speech, the others run on carrying ladders and climb up, while the drums play from behind the scenes. At the end of it, the stagekeepers fire a cannon. It makes such a loud noise that the whole building shakes. I tell you, some days it almost feels real.

Sword fights
Battle-scenes were made realistic with sword fighting. The actors were skilled sword fighters.

Fireworks
The audience loved fireworks. These could be used because the playhouse was open to the air.

The Tragicall Hiſtory
of the Life and Death
of *Doctor Fauſtus.*
Written by *Ch. Mar*

LONDON,
Printed for *Iohn Wright,* and are to be fold at his ſhop
Without Newgate, at the ſi. ... the
Bil 1636

11—Alleyn as Dr Faustus.

Dr Faustus
Christopher Marlowe's *Dr Faustus* was one of the most popular plays of the time. First performed in 1592, it was often revived over the next 50 years.

Have you ever seen a play called *Dr Faustus*? It's by Christopher Marlowe. It's about a man who has studied all the arts and sciences but still he wants to know more. So he makes a bargain with the devil. He's given great powers, but in exchange the devil will own him when he dies. So, at the end of the play, he is dragged off to hell.

When we do this here, a devil appears on the stage in a cloud of smoke. Come with me and I'll show you how it's done. Just follow me down these steps.

We're now under the stage. We call this space the hell, just as we call the roof above the stage the heavens. The devil comes down here just before he's due on stage. He waits here with two stagekeepers. Up on the stage, Dr Faustus says his magic words, the kind of words you use to call up the devil. And you must remember that the audience believe in all of this, so they're already quite nervous. When Faustus has finished, he knocks on the floor with a stick.

Now, you see that door in the roof? When the stagekeepers hear the knocking, they open it. Then the devil rushes up the ladder and jumps through the door onto the stage. As he does this, the stagekeepers set off fireworks. So it seems to the audience that he's appeared from nowhere, surrounded by smoke.

Now, I have to go and get ready. Let's go back up into the tiring house and meet some of the other actors.

Heavens
The heavens was a small roof supported by two pillars. Actors playing supernatural creatures were lowered from the heavens on a rope.

Dr Faustus is taken off to hell by a devil.

25

Men only
In Shakespeare's time it was thought that women on the stage would encourage immorality. The first actresses did not appear in plays until 1660.

Boy stars
The audience found the boy actors totally realistic. Some boys became stars in their own right. Their roles were often as long and demanding as those of the leading men.

The boy player

Hello. My name's Nick Tooley and I'm 12 years old. Since I was ten I've been living with Mr Burbage and his wife, Mistress Winifred. My own parents weren't very good to me, and I was glad when they took me in.

I'm apprenticed to Mr Burbage. That means he's teaching me how to be a player. In return, he receives my wages. The Burbages give me good meals, a bed in their house and two suits of clothes a year. It might not sound much to you, but it's a lot better than I had before. The people who work in the Globe are like a big family – well, a big, *happy* family. I had a big family before, but we weren't very happy.

My master is a wonderful teacher. He's taught me how to walk and move on the stage, and how to make myself heard all the way to the back of the playhouse. That's quite a trick, really. You have to look like you're talking in a normal voice, but everyone has to hear you.

Of course, I play mostly women's parts. It's against the law for girls or women to act on the stage. So we boys have to wear big dresses, wigs and make-up on our faces.

One day my voice is going to get deeper, and then I'll play men. In the end, I might even be famous, like Mr Burbage. Everyone's heard of him.

Every day I have lines to learn. I have a part in most of the plays we put on. I spend a lot of time in here, repeating my lines over and over.

The gallant

High fashion
Gallants' ruffs began as decorated collars and got bigger and bigger, until they were replaced by standing bands in about 1605.

On stage
The gallants sometimes paid extra money to sit on the stage. From there, they made loud comments about the play.

Allow me to introduce myself. My name is Henry Sackville. I noticed you were admiring my hat. That's an ostrich feather on top. It came all the way from Africa, so it wasn't cheap. You have to pay good money to keep up with the fashions here in London – especially if you come from a family as important as mine.

I come to the Globe every afternoon to see the other gallants (*fashionable gentlemen*) and ladies. Yes, I admit, I do like to be seen myself. I pay for my own box, which has a comfortable seat with a cushion. It's right next to the stage. But I'm not really a self-important man. I don't pay to sit on the stage itself, like some of the gallants do.

Do you like my jacket? It's called a doublet. These are real silver buttons – and there are lots of them. It's filled with horse hair to make my shoulders and arms look big and my waist look small. I used to wear a ruff (*a stiff, white folded collar*) around my neck, but this standing band is the latest thing. It's a flat collar held up by wire. There are very few of us wearing them at the moment, but I feel it is my duty to help start new fashions.

Smoking's a new fashion. In fact, I think I was the first man to light a pipe in a playhouse. The people were so surprised when I started blowing smoke. One of the groundlings shouted, "Look – the gallant's on fire."

Tobacco
Sir Walter Raleigh first brought tobacco back from America in the 1580s.

The groundling

Yes, it's true, I am a bit early – but I like coming here. There's so much to see, even before the play begins. I come some afternoons when we're not busy. My master gives me a penny – sometimes I think it's just to get me out of the way, but never mind. My master's a printer, and I'm his apprentice.

I stand in the yard here with the other apprentices, and the poorer people. We can't afford more than the penny that it costs, but we like it here. We can shout "hurrah!" and "boo!" at the different players, and if the play is boring we throw apple cores at them.

Sometimes we make fun of the rich people up in the galleries, with their expensive clothes. They call us stinkards and groundlings, but we don't care.

I like the Globe, but it's not as good as it was when Will Kemp was here. He was my favourite. He was always saying something funny. The problem was that some of the things he said hadn't been written for him. He just made them up.

Printers
London printers had been making books since 1500. Most of them sold their books near St Paul's Cathedral.

Stinkards
The gallants called the groundlings "stinkards" because their breath was said to smell bad.

This used to make Will Shakespeare angry, especially when Kemp did it in serious plays.

At the end of the play, Will Kemp used to come on and dance a jig to a pipe and a drum. He was a wonderful dancer, but he's left the Globe now. They say he argued with the other players. It's a real shame.

Will Kemp
For a bet, Will Kemp once danced 160 kilometres from London to Norwich. When he got there, he jumped over a wall to show he wasn't tired.

Rough house
The Bear Garden looked a bit like a playhouse, and even had a flag flying on top. The apprentices enjoyed the rough shows inside.

We work hard as apprentices, but we have fun too. We often play football outside the city walls. It's a rough game and there aren't many rules, so often it ends up in a fight. The Puritans would like to ban football, but they can't stop it.

I often come to Bankside because this is where most things are happening. There are bowling alleys where you try to knock down pins with a ball. A lot of the older men, the ones with money, go to places where they can play cards. And the apprentices like the Bear Garden. We can see shows of sword-fighting there and all sorts of animals. There are fights between packs of dogs and bears. People bet money on which one is going to win.

I don't mind when the bear has a chance, but when they get old, sometimes men take turns at hitting them with whips. Of course, the bear fights back and often tears the whips out of their hands. But it's not really fair, because the bear doesn't often win.

I think people who enjoy that are fairly stupid. Maybe it's because I'm in a job where I can read and write, but I like the playhouse better. I like to hear people speaking. It makes you think about things more.

Apprentices
Most London apprentices were in their late teens and early twenties. They went around in gangs and were known for their wild behaviour.

The cutpurse

What's my name? What's it got to do with you? That's what I'd like to know! You saw me doing what?

Picking that gallant's pocket? Well, he was so busy showing you his fine clothes, he was just asking for it, wasn't he? I'll tell you what, keep your mouth shut and I'll give you half the money I took from him.

You what? You want me to tell you about my life? Instead of half the money? Well, it's up to you. My name's Tom. Well, it isn't my real name, but it'll do for the moment. I'm a cutpurse – a thief who steals people's purses. I come here because it gets very crowded, but I go to other places as well – in Bankside, or across the river in the city. Wherever there are crowds of people, you'll find me – except that you won't find me, because I'm very good at not being seen.

I learned the job from the best thief in London, a gentleman called Mr Wotton. He ran a school for cutpurses – until they caught him and hanged him. That's one of the problems of the job.

I was begging in the street when Mr Wotton took me in. There were four of us boys learning to be thieves.

Easy money
People carried their money in purses tied with strings. These were in full view, which was a great help to the cutpurses.

Thief school
Mr Wotton ran a real school for cutpurses. It was discovered in 1585.

Begging words
Just like the thieves, beggars in the streets of London had a secret language of their own.

Mr Wotton used to hang a purse from the ceiling, with bells fixed onto it. We took turns trying to lift a penny from the purse without making the bells ring.

Secret names
Each thief had a name in the thieves' special language. A "curber" used a long hook to steal through windows. His lookout was called a "warp".

A hanging's a good time to steal a purse. You'd better believe this, any time they're hanging a thief, there are a dozen other thieves stealing purses from the crowd. I'm not fond of hangings, though. They remind me of where I might end up.

I think honest people go to hangings so they can feel better than the man being hanged. But I don't feel better – just a bit luckier.

I'd rather come to a playhouse, and the Globe is perfect for cutpurses. There's always a good crowd here, and the better the play, the more they watch what's happening on the stage. Sometimes we work in pairs. One of my friends pushes people in the crowd, and I go round the other side of them with my little knife.

Of course, the best purses are up there in the galleries, where the rich people sit. But you have to look like a gentleman to fit in there. Some of the older cutpurses, like the gentleman cutpurse, Mr Selman, can get away with it, but I feel much safer down here in the yard.

On Sundays, the playhouses are closed, so I might pay a visit to St Paul's Cathedral. Some of the preachers there draw big crowds. And, when people are listening to a preacher, they aren't thinking about their purses – or at least they shouldn't be. That's when I come along and help to make the rich poorer.

Well, I must be off. I have work to do. Why don't you have a chat with Kate here? She's a bit more honest than me – most of the time.

John Selman
This man was a cutpurse who dressed as a gentleman. He was caught stealing a purse at King James' court and was hanged in 1612.

Fruit gifts
Apple-sellers walked around the playhouses with baskets of fruit. Gallants often offered apples to their lady friends.

The plague

Hello. Well, he didn't stay very long – and I don't think you'll see him again. Tom doesn't like to be recognized. Me? I'm Kate Strong, the apple-seller. You must be new to town. I haven't seen you before. I'm here every day the Globe is open, and I know most of the people. But it's all going to end now, after today.

Why? Because I've just heard they're going to close the playhouses tomorrow. There's a disease called the plague and it's spreading through London again. So the flags will come down tonight, and the players will leave town.

Where will they go? Oh, around the country, to the houses of the great lords and ladies. And in between those, they'll put on shows at the inns, like they used to do. It'll be like a holiday for them. But some of us have to stay here, and it'll be hard to make a living on Bankside. The watermen will have no playgoers to carry and even the cutpurses will get hungry.

I don't know why, but the plague seems to come with the hot weather. If only a few people die, the playhouses carry on. But if there are more than 30 deaths in a week, the government closes them down. Then we have no work – or money!

London newspaper from the time of the plague.

Townspeople fleeing to the country to escape the plague.

Rats
The real cause of the plague was the flea of the black rat. The flea passed the plague on to people when it bit them.

Treatments
Some doctors rubbed patients' heads with a dead chicken. Others gave powder that they said was made from a unicorn's horn.

Nobody knows what causes the plague, but everybody's got their own ideas. Some say it's passed on by touch, others that it's caused by bad air. The preachers say it has been sent by God as a punishment for our sins. But how can that be, when it kills the preachers as well? Have they all been sinning in secret? Some even blame the playhouses. They say that going to plays leads people into sin. This makes God angry, so he sends the plague.

I don't know about this, but I do know that the plague is a horrible disease. It killed my husband two summers ago – and he was as good a man as you could hope to find. One day, he came home feeling hot and feverish, and he said he ached all over his body. He went to bed and he rolled around and sweated all night.

The next morning, I saw red swellings, as big as the apples I sell, under his arms. I knew then that it was the plague, and Jack didn't have long to live. That was a terrible night. I mean, I loved Jack and didn't want to lose him. But also, we have three children. How was I going to feed them without him to bring in some money?

We couldn't afford a doctor. But even if we could, he probably wouldn't have been able to save Jack. The doctors don't seem to know how to treat the plague. It kills the rich and the poor. May God help us all!

The only thing that can save us is winter. I hope it comes soon – the colder the better. We might freeze, but we'll stay alive. Life is hard, isn't it?

Swellings
The plague caused certain parts of the body to swell up. These swellings were called buboes, giving the disease its name, bubonic plague.

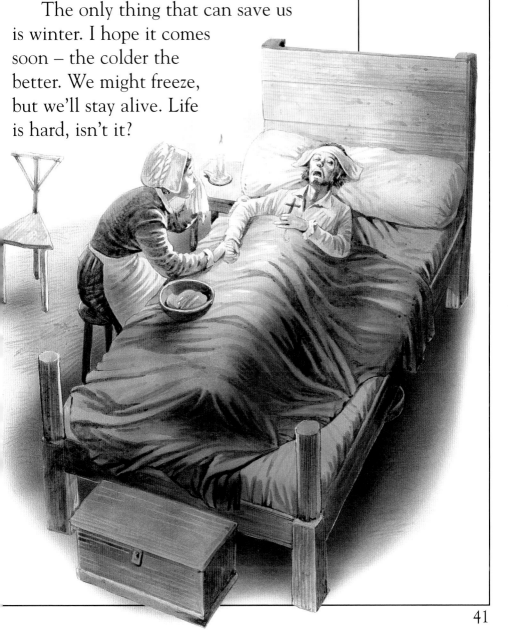

41

Henry VIII
Henry VIII was
king of England
from 1509 to
1547. He was the
father of Queen
Elizabeth.
Shakespeare's
play ends with
the birth of the
future queen.

Fire at the Globe

Eleven years have passed, and now it is an afternoon in June 1613. During that time, William Shakespeare has written some of his best plays like *Othello*, *King Lear* and *Macbeth*.

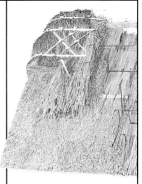

He has written one last play, *Henry VIII*, for his friends at the Globe. They are now known as "The King's Men" because their patron is James, who became king when Queen Elizabeth died. And they also have an indoor theatre at Blackfriars, where the audience is smaller, richer and better-behaved. Some players like it, but others prefer the excitement of the Globe.

For *Henry VIII*, all the effects are used. Trumpets sound, drums roll and cannons fire. Richard Burbage marches across the stage that he has made his own. Nobody notices that hot material from the cannon has risen through the air and landed on the thatched roof.

Suddenly, a shout comes from the gallery: "Fire!" The flames spread from the roof and around the playhouse. In the rush for the two narrow doors, ladies and gentlemen push against groundlings and players. Everyone escapes unhurt. The fire has taken hold now and they can only watch as the playhouse burns to the ground.

The next day, the preachers say that the fire was a sign of God's anger at playhouses. This does not stop the players making plans to rebuild the Globe.

Fire risks
The Globe was unusual because it had a thatched roof. Most buildings in 17th-century London had tiled roofs, but fires were still a danger in town.

Shakespeare and Fletcher
Shakespeare co-wrote *Henry VIII* with John Fletcher, who became the Globe's main writer after Shakespeare's death.

Second Globe
The Globe was rebuilt in less than a year. It had a fire-proof, tiled roof rather than a thatched one.

Closing the theatres

In the years after 1613, the Puritans gradually became the majority in parliament, and there was increasing tension between them and King James. He understood the Puritans very well, but his son Charles, who became king in 1625, had a different attitude. Charles simply believed that the king should rule, and that was it. In 1642, things became so bad that war broke out. Charles left London and gathered his army at Nottingham.

Parliament was now in control of London. Its leaders were strict Puritans, and now at last they got their wish. That same year, they passed a law closing the theatres and banning the performance of plays.

Oliver Cromwell (1599–1658)

This was a disaster for the players. Some performed illegally, until they were stopped by stricter laws, fines and whippings. Other players joined the king's army. The Globe's musicians played for the marching soldiers. The playhouses fell into ruin, and in 1644 the Globe was pulled down.

King Charles lost the war, and in 1649 his head was cut off. Oliver Cromwell ruled the country, at first as the head of parliament, but as time passed, more and more on his own. After he died, his son took over for a short time, but he was very weak. In the end, it was decided that there should be a king again.

Charles II came back to London from France in 1660. He loved plays and he ordered new theatres to be built. These were very different from the Globe, much more like modern theatres. They were indoors. They used artificial lighting, and painted cloths which made each scene look like a picture of real life. The actors – who now included women – performed there for small, wealthy audiences.

An age had passed. Never again in England would all classes of society go to watch new plays by the best writers.

Banning fun
The Puritans banned all kinds of fun – dancing around the maypole, football and even Christmas.

Love interest
The most famous actress of the 1660s was Nell Gwynn. King Charles fell in love with her, and she later had two sons by him.

Shakespeare today

Remains
In 1989 some underground parts of the Rose and the old Globe playhouses were discovered.

New Globe
As far as possible, the new Globe was built using the same tools, building methods and materials as the original one.

Talking Shakespeare
Whenever anyone says "tongue-tied", "vanished into thin air", or "the mind's eye", they are using Shakespeare's words.

Although the Globe was pulled down, Shakespeare's works lived on. When the new theatres opened in 1660, his were some of the first plays to be performed. His plays became so popular that they changed the English language. Every day, English speakers use phrases that he invented in the 16th century.

Shakespeare's plays have been translated into many languages. They are performed in theatres and films.

In 1987, Sam Wanamaker, the American actor and director, started to build a copy of the Globe theatre at Bankside, not far from the original site.

Ten years later, in its first season, Shakespeare's *Henry V* and *The Winter's Tale* were performed, along with works by other writers of the time. If you visit London, you can go and see a play at the Globe. You can stand in the yard like a groundling, or sit in the galleries like a gallant, just as people did then.

Hit film
One of the most popular films of 1996 was William Shakespeare's *Romeo and Juliet*, starring Leonardo de Caprio and Claire Danes. The film was set in modern times but used most of the original words.

Henry V being performed at the Globe theatre in 1997.

Modern men
The modern Globe has experimented with boys playing female roles. In 1999 the actor Mark Rylance played Cleopatra.

Glossary

acrobat
Someone who jumps, turns and walks on his or her hands to entertain an audience.

apprentices
Teenage boys and young men learning a trade e.g. shoemaking or building.

artificial
Not real. A copy of something.

attitude
A way of thinking.

audience
The people who watch a play.

balcony
A flat area you can stand on that sticks out from the wall of a house.

bargain
A contract which requires each person to agree to do something.

to brand
To make a mark on a person's or animal's skin with a piece of red-hot metal.

bowling alley
A place where people roll balls and try to knock down wooden pins.

cannon
A large gun. The older ones stood on wheels.

chat
An informal conversation.

comedy
A light-hearted play with a happy ending.

comic
Funny or amusing.

costume
The clothes an actor wears on stage.

courtyard
A piece of land surrounded by buildings or walls.

craft
A type of work, or a profession, which requires skill.

to fall into ruin
To become broken, like a very old house.

feverish
Hot and sweating because of an illness.

fireworks
Small objects with chemicals inside that burn with coloured flames or smoke, or explode, when you light them.

flag
A piece of cloth that is fixed to a pole and used as a signal.

flea
A small jumping insect that lives on the blood of animals or humans.

to fool around
To tell jokes and do silly things, in order to make people laugh.

gallery
The seated area around the inside walls of theatres like the Globe.

globe
Another name for the world.

hanging
Killing a criminal by tightening a rope around the neck.

illegally
Without permission and against the law.

immorality
Behaviour that is morally wrong.

inn
An old word for a hotel.

jig
A dance to the pipe and drum.